BUFFER ZONE: SNAPSHOTS FROM AN ABORTION CLINIC ESCORT

Christine Taylor

Buffer Zone: Snapshots from an Abortion Clinic Escort ©**2020** by **Christine Taylor**. Published in the United States by Vegetarian Alcoholic Press. Not one part of this work may be reproduced without expressed written consent from the author. For more information, please contact vegalpress@gmail.com

Cover Art by Eleanor Hazard

For those who support the right to choose and defend access to safe, legal, and accessible abortion services.

Table of Contents

Hell Sent Me a Greeting Card
    5
Jesus Loves the Babies
    6
The Escort Files: A Zuihitsu
    7
The Holy Bible, Appendix B
    11
Buffer Zone
    12
An Abortion Clinic Escort's Dolores Umbridge
    13
"Hands Up, Don't Abort!"
    15
Sticks & Stones
    16
Ode to Plastic Jesus
    17
Haiku
    18
Homage to My Middle-Aged Black Body
    19
Then the Flood
    20
Self-Care
    21
Gauntlet
    22
When They Come
    23
To My Fellow Clinic Escorts: Englewood, NJ
    26

Hell Sent Me a Greeting Card

According to the screamers, we escorts
are *purveyors of death in a culture that loves death*:
Valentine hearts around skulls with X'ed out eyes
chocolate-covered cherries that spew blood when bitten

I love when I can't breathe. . .

a missed step
on the sidewalk
I'm blocked by the mob of antis
a patient struggles
through snarling mouths
groping hands
to the door.

I need to be faster.

Jesus Loves the Babies

The rain doesn't keep the protesters away,
the sidewalk in front of the library
across the street from the women's clinic
is lined with the usuals:
Korean Catholics
white Evangelicals.
A woman in a long dark dress belted at the waist
pushes a hooded baby carriage up the sidewalk
joins the crowd.
I have never seen her here before–
who brings out an infant in a torrent of rain?

As she bounces the swaddled baby
under her large dome umbrella
the limbs don't move
the head remains oddly still. . .
a plastic baby doll like I had in the 80s
one that does pee-pee after her bottle
the mouth an endless pucker
waiting for a rush down its throat.

While she soothes her baby,
pats the doll's back, kisses its molded forehead,
the rain pauses
and one of the other escorts looks up at the sky.

The clouds take no shape.

The Escort Files: A Zuihitsu

This morning the temperature is 13°F. My double-wall vacuum-insulated Klean Kanteen will be put to the test. I paid $19.99 for it at Whole Foods and am still questioning the purchase.

+

One of the regular screamers asks if we know how many abortions are performed each day. Propped against his gut is a sign bearing a magnified image of a bloody fetus with the caption "3,500 Babies Murdered Every Day," so I'm gonna take a guess that the number is not 3,500. The *New England Journal of Medicine* cites 3,700; the CDC reports just under 1,800. My co-escort says she can't take that sign seriously because the intestines look like ramen.

+

When the runner approaches where he's standing near the clinic door, he whispers 29. She nods. Mutters a Hail Mary as her white pearl rosary slips through her fingers.

+

grace
/grās/
noun
1. simple elegance or refinement of movement.
2. (in Christian belief) the free and unmerited favor of God, as manifested in the salvation of sinners and the bestowal of blessings.

verb
1. do honor or credit to (someone or something) by one's presence.

+

She must have been on vacation–it's been weeks–but today, she's back. In those fucking suede wedgie boots. She begins the chase, runs after patients all the way to the door, leans over my shoulder. I shrug her off, and she shouts, "Moms deserve love and support–it's never too late to change your mind!" Once the clinic doors close, she turns, gets so close to my face that my eyes feel crossed, tells me that she has a right to educate women. Her lawyer says we are not to get in her way.

+

According to several sources I Google on my iPhone, tigers are one of the world's top apex predators with no natural enemies. They exist at the top of their food chain.

+

Q-Tip arrives in her signature furry white hat and fur-lined snow boots. A small American flag is haphazardly attached with duct tape to the sign around her neck. "Jesus loves the babies! Jesus LOVES THE BABIES!"

+

ice shards
in a sidewalk crack
holy redeemer

+

Despite the HotHands toe warmers, my feet have gone numb. I know the tingling will remain after I bathe this afternoon.

+

The Mayo Clinic says that there are four stages of frostbite. During the last stage, "the area turns black and hard as the tissue dies."

+

The antis laugh at a companion who's having a cigarette on the sidewalk. Say he's strung out on heroin. Say he's the worst kind of sinner. As he raises the cigarette to his lips, his shaky hand zig-zags the smoke. Three antis surround him, and then the screaming. Pink vests swoop in, and I threaten to call the cops. Say I'm always calling the cops. Say I'm always trying to persecute them. Say they have a right to free speech. Say I should be calling the cops on the druggie-loser. He's crying now. Rubs his brow. Looks up at the clinic window. Says he just wants some peace.

+

"Peace be with you, and also with you."

+

The sidewalk a proscenium stage:
"Our Lady of the Theatre" challenges the screamers,
what about lesbians? why can't they adopt babies?
in her bedraggled clothing
cookbooks from the library under her arm
she withstands their eruption
live oak in a hurricane
Men, men, men, men, men... everything men!

When she is here, they don't see me.

+

Two more planters boasting decorative pine have appeared on the sidewalk. The restaurant next door must really be in the Christmas spirit. I try to move them to make room for patients to walk to the clinic door, but they won't budge.

+

gaunt·let²
/ˈgôntlət,ˈgäntlət/
noun
1. go through an intimidating or dangerous crowd, place, or experience in order to reach a goal.
2. undergo the military punishment of receiving blows while running between two rows of men with sticks.

+

"Women were not made to be rulers!"

+

At the end of the shift, I climb the long hill to my car on the street lined with Victorian houses; on Saturdays, the parking is free. While I adjust Spotify to find the right playlist for the long ride home, one of the screamers–the guy with the creepy Hitler-mustache–walks by on the sidewalk. As he passes the window, we stare at each other. He looks away first. I watch him in the rear-view mirror until he saunters out of sight. He never looks back.

+

Her baby was already dead.

+

He returns from the diner, whispers to the escorts that in five minutes we need to take cover. From the recessed driveway, we hear the thud of hard-boiled eggs hurled at their signs. Another time, a companion who's carrying almost makes good. Another time, the security guards circle the building when an unknown bag propped against the building shows up on camera. Another time. . .

+

Hot coffee escapes
my mouth
dribbles down my chin

stains my collar.

The Holy Bible, Appendix B

Faithful disciples of the Bread of Life Church
arrive to deliver the good word.
Today, the men have brought their wives and children
lined strollers along the curb
in front of the women's clinic
hung signs bearing images of bloody fetuses
around the necks of their five-year-olds
whose jackets look too thin for the cold.

The Holy Bible says
we are to love our neighbor perfectly
and Democrats are dividing us
confusing God's plan
making women think that this is about health care.

Heads nod, hands clap
and my co-escort rubs her eyes.
I watch the women with their children
remember the book of Bible stories
my mother read me before bed
the illustration of Jonah in the whale's belly
I can't remember
how he survived being swallowed whole. . .

One of the mothers whispers in her child's ear
points at the clinic door
and when the next patient approaches
the child runs up to her
wraps his little body around her legs
begs, "Please don't kill me!"

To love God perfectly
is the sum of His commandments.

filed the lawsuit challenging the protest-free buffer zones around the facilities in 2015

defendant cannot make a good-faith argument

escalated from quiet vigils

shouting at patients

yelling

disappointed

Englewood did not prosecute the individuals for their actions outside the clinic

defendant created a sweeping regulation that burdens the free speech of individuals

restricted

double standard

address the contentious protests outside the clinic

Abortion clinic buffer zone in Englewood struck down by federal judge

so invasive

antiabortion advocate

distribute literature and rosaries

Megan Burrow, Staff Writer, @MegBurrow Published 4:33 a.m. ET Nov. 21, 2017 | Updated 12:22 p.m. ET Nov. 21, 2017

"Defendant did not create a targeted statute to address the specific issue of congestion or militant and aggressive protesters outside of the clinic"

confrontations on the sidewalk

the city attorney could not be reached for comment

city failed to show that it tried less restrictive measures

8-foot space on either side of medical office doors was to protect patients from protesters yelling and grabbing at them

overjoyed when the council understood what this meant for the patients

sad result

the measure violates their rights of free speech and free assembly under the First Amendment

An Abortion Clinic Escort's Dolores Umbridge

Traffic clamors
up Engle Street.

She arrives in her sparkly white
Mercedes Benz convertible
parks across the street from the clinic.
From the trunk, she retrieves
her toolkit: a canvas fanny-pack stuffed
with strings of cheap blue rosary beads
plastic fetus dolls
pamphlets for Rachel's Vineyard.

She is doing God's work
chasing patients
from their cars to the door
her voice gossamer
over my shoulder
as I escort a patient
tangled in a web of self-doubt
her scurrying alongside
shoving beads
shoving dolls
shoving pamphlets

Moms deserve love and support, not abortion!

When I take the patient's shaking hand
her skin is cold.
So is mine.

The sidewalk is uneven.

Once the clinic door closes
I turn and meet her face
small upturned nose
shell-pink lips
the soft lines of her cheeks
a kindness that collects–

I'd rather the screamers
with their filth and vitriol
the prating about sinners and Jesus
the taunts over Margaret Sanger
the posters of mutilated bodies and blood

at least I know what I'm getting.

She is doing God's work
chasing patients
from the door to their cars
her voice honey
over my shoulder
as I escort a patient
limbs heavy
her scurrying behind
offering support
offering prayer
offering forgiveness

    God loves you, and He can help you!

When I take the patient's trembling hand
a moan rumbles deep in her throat.
My gut quakes.

The tree hangs too low.

Across the street from the clinic
into the trunk of her sparkly white
Mercedes Benz convertible
she stuffs her toolkit
covers the blue rosary beads
plastic fetus dolls
pamphlets
with a wide-brimmed sun hat.

The engine purrs
down the one-way street.

"Hands Up, Don't Abort!"

Bold caption
on the protester's sign
a smiling toddler
skin brown
like mine
hands raised
toward the shining
light of the camera
reaching
for someone
he loves
for someone
who loves him.

In twenty years
when he is a man
he will again reach
towards a shining light
this time
at the end
of a slick baton
he will hope
beyond reason
he is reaching
for the love
of a country..

When he puts
his hands up
they won't
abort.

Sticks & Stones

He takes his usual place on the sidewalk directly in front
of the clinic door, adjusts his microphone, the amplifier screeches
to life. He begins his preaching, "It's a terrible day out here
in Englewood where babies are being murdered!" I'm stationed
at the door, and already my ears are ringing. I take a swig
of coffee from my thermos, the movement triggers him, he goes on
about the escorts having better things to do on a Saturday, like
going to *Poetry Out Loud* in Morristown, a reference so specific,
the press release written when a student I advised won the regional
competition some months ago, the two of us smiling in victory
on stage in photographs.

I wonder how much research he had to do to find this obscure
tidbit, such a grotesque fascination with me that has gone
into sharpening a dagger to pierce me, unnerve me, rock
my foundation. I wonder if he stayed up late clicking away
at a computer with a bad Wi-Fi connection, the triumph
he must have felt unearthing this nugget. I wonder how I appeared
in his imagination at the uncovering, how I must have buckled.
Was I on my knees?

As I stand at the door, staring across the street at the library,
he reveals that he knows my name. Like all predators, he watches
for my reaction: he wants me panicky, wants me vulnerable, wants
me naked before him in truth. I don't flinch. And we all know
what happens when men don't get what they want.

A patient and her companion navigate the sidewalk, the team tries
to keep the screamers and the runner at bay. We daisy-chain
the space leading to the door, get them safely inside. As I close
the door, he's right behind me–a mountain of a man–his amplified
words reach like claws. I turn, and for an eternal second, I look
into his eyes, puffy and watery, foul ponds that turn up dead fish.
He backs away, the sole of his shoe catches the concrete, and he
slams down his poster bearing a bloody fetus for support. He has
seen it. . . he has seen it. . . death looking him right in the eye.
And he's pointing at me and screaming about Satan's black
bodyguard paving the way for evil.

And there I am under the arch of the door, all five feet of me
in my pink vest, traffic rumbling down the one-way street,
and like a stampede of wild horses comes the laughter.

Ode to Plastic Jesus

To forgive us our sins,
oh Lord,
they have brought you here
across the street
from the women's clinic
this rainy Saturday morning,
propped you up against
the legs of one of your disciples
in full splendor:
a gilded, ornately carved frame
bearing an oil painting
of your likeness
carefully Saran-wrapped
to protect you from the elements.
Oh Lord, forgive us our trespasses
as we escort women
through the pro-lifers' amplified onslaught,
Stand up for your baby, Mom!
They rip babies out of the womb
limb by limb!
You're all sinners
fornicators
murderers!
Forgive us for seeking safe entry,
for stumbling
on uneven pavement.
Lord, I know you hear our prayer–
a patient clutches my vest
cries on my shoulder,
while rain slides down slick plastic
pools in a sidewalk crack.
Deliver us.

				These Deathscorts work for Satan!
	Please come out–we can help you!

				It's a terrible day here on Engle Street,
					where babies are being murdered!
These doctors just want your money!
		So many couples would be happy to adopt your baby!
			I pray today that you cry out to God!
	All the body parts are in place
		7 weeks after conception!
						There's life inside you!
			God hates the hand that sheds innocent blood!

What are you going to do on the day of Judgement?
						Sinners repent!

	We can offer you free services!		**through the din**
							sunlight floods
	Be a man, Dad!				**the horizon**		Jesus, Lord of Light!

					You've got the blood of babies on you!
She deserves the wrath of a just God!
				We are not here because of self-righteousness–
		we are here because we have all been filthy
			in our sins and needed a savior!

					Trust in Jesus Christ!
	Come to Jesus Christ and be saved
		to walk in the newness of life!

				This is the gospel of grace!
		God can change your heart, but you don't trust God!
The Lord will provide!
					A child is a gift from the Lord!
			Judgement is upon you!

Homage to My Middle-Aged Black Body

Because most of the time I hate this body
stiff hip flexors, cracking knees
sore, cystic breasts
rolls and stretch marks
that appear in mirrored angles

I marvel when on the sidewalk
escorting at the women's clinic
I swell by how completely I love this body
the brownness of it
its animal-like awareness, its speed getting to patients
the thickness of its thighs
the hip-switch in perfect-boot-cut jeans
the full ass that pushes antis out of the way
the magic that creates me giant
a force.

Despite all its failings
that this body can be a shield
deflecting *Come to Lord Jesus Christ and be saved,*
Walk in the newness of Life!
off my back
mighty like myth
legs spread
arms triangling out to my fellow escorts
the daisy chain we create
to bloom safety on the sidewalk
raptures me–
I hug my jacket more snugly around my core
tuck the loose ends of my T-shirt into my jeans
to keep warm.

Later, when I'm small again
scraping anxious fingernails
across wrinkled skin on my hands
I'll try to recapture this feeling
of magnanimity
claw at the height of this other self
wonder at the price I've paid for it.

Then the Flood

Already the rain threatens–
my tires graze pools of water
as I make my way up I-95.

Outside the clinic, the "ambassadors of Heaven"
scream on crackled amplifiers
but the rain has its own plans
soon fat drops soak through my umbrella
the water seems determined to wash away the filth
and within minutes the street floods.

When flash-flood warnings buzz on our phones
I don't tell my team I'm terrified
of being trapped, or worse, drowned–
another patient and her companion are coming
so we trudge through the current
that has already passed our ankles
the screamers shout we "need to surrender to the living God Jesus
Christ" and all I can imagine is our being swept away
water carrying us to some swampy ditch in Secaucus
where we'll flounder in muck.

Then he hits me with a sign that reads "God Gives Eternal Life"
leans in close
his breath rises in the cold like smoke from a wasteland on fire
whispers that he can end me

    & I remember being in the dark
choked in a drunken rage
                  by the one who promised to love me most
          stale whiskey breath hot on my face
     & the pounding, I thought my head would explode
I slipped away on a river
              there were so many stars. . .

Yet I'm still so much here.

I blow him a kiss
that sends him into a fit
surround a patient with my arms
tell her, "Good morning."

Self-Care

after the shift
i sink into the bathtub
steam fogs the mirror

the cat wails
from the edge of the tub
his eyes bright
though his body is wracked with age

he implores for answers
i don't have

my head splits

the water nearly scalds
palms pink

these hands that never come clean

Gauntlet

you remember that day almost two decades ago //
    vomiting that refused to be restricted to only mornings //
        the car turned the corner to a horde //
they lined the streets then too //
    you looked away from their signs //
        the one with the dismembered arm, the hand reaching out to. . . //

car parked, your hand trembled on the door handle //
        a smiling man approached, helped you onto the sidewalk //
he was older and white //
    he wore a bright yellow vest, like that of a crossing guard //
        you can't remember the details of his face //
        his hair silver, longer than most men wear at that age //
    and he was tall //

he pressed your head to his chest //
        covered your ear with his warm palm //
    told you not to listen //
     Hell is waiting for you! //
        God is the Father of everlasting life! //
            repent, murderer! //
    the voices melted into the hum of his heartbeat //

an open door

in the waiting room, magazines of *Better Homes and Gardens* //
    your partner's fingers laced in yours //
        the garnet in your class ring faintly glinted like wine //
    you waited for your name to be called //

you know you loved too well

When They Come

Their minivans arrive at 7:45 a.m., the blue "Free Sonogram" van follows
a white dove, wings arched to Heaven, painted on the door
and they park directly across the street.

They never pay the meters.

Today, they have come with an extra car
a dented red station wagon bearing out-of-state plates.
We escorts watch as one, two. . . seven men crawl out of the backseat.
Through patches of clouds, sunlight dapples the road
and pigeons peck day-old bread from the sidewalk in front of the diner.

Another Saturday morning at the women's clinic.

The men take turns on the microphone
gospel and filth amplified to illegal decibels
we are fornicators
we are murderers
we are Hitler's ignorant fools.
Up next one of the new guys
tall, thin, bald, sharp facial angles & cavernous shadows
eyes undead blue
and when he preaches, he is articulate
unlike the other screamers who bark about sinners and Jesus.

Mid-morning, the patient-pool lags
so the men want to engage.
And we're here
in our neon pink escort vests.
They walk up.
We ignore them.

But they are men
        who must be heard.

My partner Lola has her hair in Pippi Longstocking braids
and I focus on the elastic-tied ends
as they surround us
and the tall one is saying something about sin
& sex
& murder
& Jesus.

He asks if I know. . .

   I swat a fly buzzing near my face

 Do you know?

my eyes water
so Lola starts talking to me

   & her hands are flitting

& I turn my back to him
  talk about birds weather
     the comeback of My Little Pony

& it's hot
   & it smells like garbage

    & *sinners*

& Lola's lips are so red

    & I don't know what she's saying
     [I think roller derby]

 & *Jesus.*

   & what the fuck am I saying?

& all I see are her lips
  full.

When he snakes his body around mine,
I feel the moist heat of his breath on my neck
as he whispers,
You know, you're a dirty girl.

And last night your breath on my neck
    the bite took my breath away. . .

And I'm choking on stuck words
     and there are patients coming. . .

Your fingers laced my neck
  choking
    candlelight
  shadows
    my leg shaking. . .

Do you know?

    Do you know?

I know.

I know I'm a dirty girl.

This morning's bitter coffee bubbles in the wicked cauldron of my gut
and I swallow
    I have to hold it down
because there are patients trying to cross the street
and I need to escort them
wearing my pink vest I stop traffic
tires screech
    bile burns my throat.

And it's loud
& it's hot
& it's hard to breathe. . .

    Somewhere in me a city's on fire.

And those undead eyes are watching.

Later, he sits next to me on the stone half-wall
my legs dangle over the edge, his firmly planted
and from the Snapware container I take to school every morning,
I offer him an unwashed grape
the fruit firm, green
newly ripe.

After the shift, I drive home.
And shower.
And crawl into bed.

& dream

To My Fellow Clinic Escorts: Englewood, NJ

May you arrive at the clinic promptly at 7:30 a.m.–the first patients
come early for their 8 o'clock appointments even in rain and snow.
May you don a neon vest, reflective panels glittering in the rising sun,
wear this "Deathscort" badge with honor and pride. May you stop
traffic that tears up the one-way downtown drag, usher her safely
to the curb. May you hold her hand and open the door. May you lift
your head towards the open sky when a protester wails
on his amplifier, "I feel sorry for my brother who has to bear the burden
of being an innocent white man," after a pedestrian has called the cops,
again, your laughter will quake the heavens. May you pop that Advil
you've stashed in your jeans pocket, and no, it doesn't matter
that you've already downed three cups of bitter black coffee.
Please get out of the buffer zone. May you swallow the memories
of your own past assault(s), body-check the bastard who's trying
to slip a patient a pamphlet of false promises (*We'll care for you
and your baby!*), watch out for the pothole in the sidewalk
that catches garbage-water when they dump the bins. May you
just listen to the story she tells: the struggle to feed other children
when dad's been laid off, the first-generation college degree
in arm's reach, the tumor that has claimed 70% of the fetus;
each story becomes your own. May you fall to your knees
when you hear that "God has called women to be submissive
to their godly leaders" and praise the Mother Goddess
as we bear witness to the choice to honor life, the heart
of these journeys. Down the street, sirens.

Acknowledgements

Many thanks to the following journals in which these poems originally appeared:

Jesus Loves the Babies, *Anti-Heroin Chic*

The Holy Bible, Appendix B, *Juke Joint Magazine*

An Abortion Clinic Escort's Dolores Umbridge, *Rag Queen Periodical*

Sticks & Stones, *Anti-Heroin Chic*

Homage to My Middle-Aged Black Body, *Elephants Never*

Then the Flood, *Ghost City Review*

Self-Care, *Anti-Heroin Chic*

When They Come, *Glass Poetry: Poets Resist*

To My Fellow Clinic Escorts: Englewood, NJ, *Glass Poetry: Poets Resist*

www.ingramcontent.com/pod-product-compliance
Lightning Source LLC
Chambersburg PA
CBHW030142100526
44592CB00011B/1013